HISTORIC IMAGES OF THE
ADIRONDACKS

HISTORIC IMAGES OF THE
ADIRONDACKS

From the Collection of the

ADIRONDACK MUSEUM

COMPILED BY VICTORIA VERNER SANDIFORD

ADIRONDACK MUSEUM
Blue Mountain Lake, New York

NORTH COUNTRY BOOKS, INC.
Utica, New York

Historic Images of the Adirondacks
Copyright © 2008
by the Adirondack Museum & North Country Books

Design by Zach Steffen & Rob Igoe, Jr.

ISBN-10 1-59531-016-9
ISBN-13 978-1-59531-016-3

Library of Congress Cataloging-in-Publication Data

Sandiford, Victoria Verner.
  Historic images of the Adirondacks : from the collection of the Adirondack Museum / compiled
by Victoria Verner Sandiford.
      p. cm.
  ISBN-13: 978-1-59531-016-3 (alk. paper)
  ISBN-10: 1-59531-016-9 (alk. paper)
  1. Adirondack Mountains (N.Y.)--History--Pictorial works. I. Adirondack Museum. II. Title.
  F127.A2S26 2008
  974.7'500222--dc22
                                        2008042514

ADIRONDACK MUSEUM   NORTH COUNTRY BOOKS, INC.
P.O. Box 99, Routes 28N & 30   220 Lafayette Street
Blue Mountain Lake, New York 12812   Utica, New York 13502

CONTENTS

VINTAGE PHOTOBELT, ADIRONDACK MUSEUM, 1960S

FOREWORD

The Adirondack Museum is a collection of regional history and art located in Blue Mountain Lake, New York. The museum explores and presents the story of the Adirondacks, the place and its people, mounting exhibitions, offering programs, and sponsoring publications that bring Adirondack history to life.

Since its inception in 1957, the museum has collected historical and cultural artifacts that document the complex interaction between people and wilderness. Among the most significant are those that make up the Historic Photograph Collection. More than most images, photographs have the power to capture the beautiful and the ravaged, the powerful and the weak, work and play. This volume highlights images from the museum's collection that illuminate our collective past, help explain the present, and perhaps, hopefully, point to a direction for the future.

—Caroline M. Welsh, Director

ACKNOWLEDGMENTS

Putting together a photograph album at home has its own challenges. Which group shot from the family vacation should go in? There are ten photos of Grandma with little Arthur. Should they all go in? Celebrations, vacations, and lifestyles are documented through the eyes of the camera and tucked away until there is a rainy day to mount them into an album. Compiling a book of photographs from the Adirondack Museum's collection is yet more challenging and wouldn't have been possible without the help of many friends.

Edward Comstock's knowledge of the region and the museum's photograph collection, along with his constant urging to dig deeper, helped shape this book. Together, we looked at over five thousand images, but it was impossible to include every town and village in the Adirondack Park.

This book wouldn't have come to fruition without the assistance of Angela Donnelly Snye, the Museum's Assistant Curator. Her ability to hunt and find photographs and add fresh ideas of her own made the project fun and full of discovery.

Special thanks go to Caroline M. Welsh, Director of the Museum. Her support of the project allowed me to take the reins and run. Special thanks go to Joan Demarsh, Associate Manager of Retail Operations, for listening, looking, and suggesting, to Laura Rice and Jerry Pepper for their contributions, to Rob Igoe, Jr., and Zach Steffen of North Country Books for their patience, to Micaela Hall and Christine Campeau for letting me dig through the boxes of photos that they use for teaching, and to Debbie Austin and Erin Harper for assistance with organizing the boxes of Xeroxed photos—not an easy job.

Very special thanks to my father, William K. Verner, whose love for this wilderness was passed on to me.

For William and Henry.

Victoria Verner Sandiford
August 12, 2008
Long Lake, NY

INTRODUCTION

This book celebrates more than one hundred fifty years of life in New York State's Adirondack Mountains. Through its photographic images, the reader has the opportunity to see people and places that have long since disappeared: an immense pile of pulpwood in Newton Falls, Georgia O'Keefe summering in Lake George, a small mom-and-pop general store and post office in Newcomb. Other photos depict places that are still familiar parts of the landscape: Camp Pine Knot, Fish Creek Pond Campsite, and the Ausable Chasm, for example, can still be visited and appreciated today. Individually, each of these photographs offers a glimpse of a single moment in time; together, they form a visual history of the Adirondacks.

The two hundred images contained within this book represent only a small portion of the Adirondack Museum's more than eighty thousand photographs and negatives. Compiler Victoria Sandiford has drawn from this vast collection, including works by professional photographers, private photos from family albums, and images of cabinet cards, real photo postcards, stereoviews, and snapshots. They document the landscape, buildings, roads, villages, and hamlets of the Adirondack Park. More importantly, they represent the community of people who shaped this region.

Some of the images present a gritty view of life in the Adirondacks. During much of the nineteenth century, the region was valued as a source of lumber and mineral ores. An anonymous photographer captured a group of six men posing with their peavies and cant hooks atop a sea of logs near Glens Falls in about 1890. They are there to sort the logs by hand before they are sent to a mill for processing. The sheer number of logs is staggering: the waters of the Hudson River are completely obscured, a testament to the extent of logging activities in the Adirondack Mountains.

Mining also brought people to the region to extract minerals and ores. More than two hundred fifty mines and processing sites were established to remove eleven different minerals: iron, lead, garnet, talc, graphite, copper, zinc, pyrite, feldspar, wollastonite, and titanium. By 1840, nearly thirty Adirondack towns had grown up around iron mining or processing.

In 1891, Seneca Ray Stoddard photographed a group of children watching the beehive-shaped charcoal kilns lining the shores of Chateaugay Lake as they consumed Adirondack hardwood to create fuel for iron forges. In 1910, photographer Ernest Ameden documented men and machines at the Barton and Hooper garnet mines in North River and published them as real photo postcards. In one, a worker pauses from stoking the engine of a steam shovel in a pit to pose in the machine's doorway, his face and clothes streaked with grime.

These depictions of heavy industry in the Adirondacks may not seem appealing to the modern eye but to nineteenth and early twentieth century viewers, they represented progress and enterprise, and a reasonable use of the land's bountiful resources.

The Adirondacks were, of course, also valued for spectacular scenery, fresh air, and recreational opportunities. As industry produced roads and rail transportation to move raw materials and supplies, people soon followed. Some came for their health, to "cure" in the balsam-scented air. Most came to escape the heat and stresses of urban life, seeking fun and adventure. Photographers documented the fashionable resorts and hunting camps that attracted thousands of these city-weary visitors to the woods.

Tourists wishing for mementos of their summer adventures were a ready market for cabinet cards, real photo postcards, and stereoviews. These souvenirs, brought home and shared with friends and family, also served to advertise the region, further spurring the popularity of the Adirondacks as a resort destination. Some of these views are iconic: hundreds of fish caught on one outing, a guideboat on the shore of a scenic lake, a grizzled guide holding a rifle or carrying a boat on his shoulders.

In 1900, George Eastman introduced the Brownie camera, and photography became a do-it-yourself activity. Photographs became spontaneous and more intimate, as tourists, campers, and sportsmen and women created their own visual records of their Adirondack adventures. Hikers from Putnam Camp spelled out "MARCY" with their bodies at the summit in 1902. In 1925, environmental advocate Bob Marshall mugged for the camera next to a fallen directional sign for Mt. Marcy. Even "French Louie," guide and Adirondack character, agreed to be photographed by visiting "sports" as part of the local color.

Throughout the nineteenth and early twentieth centuries, photographers documented the landscape and the people who lived, worked, and played in the Adirondacks. Their cameras recorded the trains, steamboats, and wagons that brought them; the camps and hotels that housed them; the explorers, miners, loggers, hunters, and settlers; the harsh realities of a subsistence living for some alongside the luxury that surrounded others. Their images captured the beauties of the landscape: the mountains, lakes, rivers, woods, and incredible vistas. The Adirondacks they photographed was by turns wild and woolly, gritty and hardscrabble, breathtakingly beautiful and awe inspiring. There was an Adirondack Park to suit every taste.

These images helped persuade New Yorkers to value and preserve the Adirondack wilderness for its wild beauty, restorative powers, and vast resources. Images of Adirondack people, communities, and landscapes helped foster a sense of place among those who lived and played in the region. More than a mere record of what things looked like, the Adirondack Museum's Historic Photograph Collection is a mirror of the hopes, dreams, and imaginings of New Yorkers past and a window through which to view the life of an American wilderness.

—Laura S. Rice, Chief Curator

LAKE GEORGE
REGION

**"ON THE PLANK," FRENCH MOUNTAIN, HALFWAY BETWEEN
GLENS FALLS AND LAKE GEORGE TOLL GATE**
Lake George, 1879, Seneca Ray Stoddard, P010831

SAMUEL J. WAGSTAFF AND COMPANY
Lake George, 1890, L.H. Filmore, P010845

MORNING EXERCISE AT CAMP REDWING, A CHILDREN'S SUMMER CAMP
Schroon Lake, ca 1925, Eastern Illustrating Co., P013425

FORT WILLIAM HENRY HOTEL
Lake George, ca 1890, Seneca Ray Stoddard, P001515

HULETT'S LANDING
Lake George, ca 1885, Seneca Ray Stoddard, P001398

HULETT'S LANDING WALKWAY
Lake George, 1871, Seneca Ray Stoddard, P027728

HULETT'S LANDING WITH HULETT'S HOUSE IN BACKGROUND
Lake George, 1889, Seneca Ray Stoddard, P001402

HORICON PAVILION DINING ROOM
Lake George, ca 1890, P001517

SILVER BAY HOUSE
Lake George, ca 1902, Seneca Ray Stoddard, P027059

ROGER'S SLIDE
Lake George, ca 1895, P032982

ARTIST GEORGIA O'KEEFE AT OAKLAWN
Lake George, 1918, Alfred Stieglitz, P061445

AT AN AMERICAN CANOE ASSOCIATION MEET
Lake George, 1892, L.H. Filmore, P010851

THE WAYSIDE HOTEL, LUZERNE
Lake Luzerne, ca 1890, Seneca Ray Stoddard, P001336

MAIN STREET, WARRENSBURG, GATEWAY TO THE ADIRONDACKS
Warrensburg, ca 1890, P000044

SHIRT FACTORY
Warrensburg, ca 1890, P000043

TALLY-HO LEAVING POTTERSVILLE LANDING ON SCHROON LAKE
Schroon Lake, ca 1900, James Shaughnessy, P014378

BRACE DAM ON BOREAS RIVER
Schroon Lake, 1908, Norman Stewart Foote, P023317

MIDGET'S BUNGALOWS AT CAMP WAKONDA
Pottersville, ca 1925, Eastern Illustrating Co., P013926

WATER SPORTS AT CAMP RONDACK
Pottersville, ca 1920, Eastern Illustrating Co., P013884

WELLS HOUSE
Pottersville, ca 1895, P049198

S.S. *EVELYN* AT POTTERSVILLE LANDING ON SCHROON LAKE
Pottersville, ca 1890, P042628

NORTH CREEK REGION

JOHNSBURG TAXIDERMIST
Johnsburg, ca 1880, Osmond Putnam, P024240

THE MARION HOUSE, A FRIENDS LAKE HOTEL, CHESTERTOWN
Friends Lake, ca 1910, Eastern Illustrating Co., P012026

CAMP ROGERS
Friends Lake, ca 1900, P023541

NORTH CREEK STATION
North Creek, 1880, J.F. Holley, P001026

FRANK HOOPER'S FIRST GARNET MINE IN THE TOWNSHIP
North Creek, ca 1890, P038161

LOGS ON SKIDS, MAIN STREET
North Creek, ca 1910, P000203

ICE BLOCKADE IN ROAD
North Creek, 1909, Ernest J. Ameden, P017036

SKIERS TRAVELING FROM THE TRAIN DEPOT TO THE SKI SLOPE
North Creek, 1932, P050015

A HORSE-DRAWN SLEIGH IN A TUNNEL CARVED THROUGH THE SNOW
Minerva, ca 1910, Eastern Illustrating Co., P070179

WILLIAM NYLAN AT THE MINERVA HOTEL
Minerva, 1908, P011360

**STEAM SHOVEL AT
THE BARTON MINE**
North River, 1920, P046032

BARTON MINE
North River, 1920, Ernest J. Ameden, P046031

CAR OF ROCK HEADED TO CONCENTRATION PILE, BARTON MINE
North River, 1920, Ernest J. Ameden, P046034

FAMOUS OLD NASSAU BAR AT FARRELL'S TAVERN
Indian Lake, ca 1960, 1986.024.007

**INDIAN LAKE ROAD
AT LEWEY LAKE**
*Indian Lake, ca 1930,
Frederick A. Hodges, P060461*

THE CEDARS
Indian Lake, ca 1930, Eastern Illustrating Co., P012190

H.A. APALMATIER & CO. GENERAL MERCHANDISE
Indian Lake, 1914, P020039

HORSES AND WAGON CROSSING THE CEDAR RIVER ON A LOG FERRY
Indian Lake, ca 1890, P007202

LOUIS "FRENCH LOUIE" SEYMOUR IN FRONT OF HIS HOME
West Canada Lakes, ca 1895, P008154

BATHING BEACH AT CAMP OF THE WOODS
Speculator, ca 1910, P023520

CAMP OF THE WOODS
Speculator, ca 1930, P060451

CAMP OF THE WOODS, BEACH CAMPING ON LAKE PLEASANT
Speculator, ca 1930, P060454

OLD FORGE REGION

GRIDLEY'S CABINS & RESTAURANT
Otter Lake, 1921, Eastern Illustrating Co., P012618

LIGHTHOUSE CABINS
Otter Lake, ca 1945,
P035598

WAITING FOR THE TRAIN, FULTON CHAIN STATION
Thendara, ca 1910, Henry M. Beach, P017095

RAILROAD STATION
Thendara, ca 1900,
Henry M. Beach,
P005432

ADIRONDACK LEAGUE CLUB MOUNTAIN LODGE
Old Forge, ca 1910, Henry M. Beach, P002160

OLLIE TUTTLE,
INVENTOR OF THE "DEVIL
BUG" FISHING LURE
Old Forge, 1919, P008178

ST. BARTHOLOMEW'S CHURCH
Old Forge, ca 1920,
Henry M. Beach, P017051

CHIEF DENNIS AND FAMILY MAKING BASKETS
Old Forge, ca 1920, P042065

AMERICAN LEGION BASEBALL TEAM: BUM GIMLICK, DON CASE, ART TICKNER, WALLEY FARMER, BURDIE DEIS, CLARK WOODRUFF, STUB GALLAGER, FATHER McNEAL, JACK DUNN, CHARLIE BRICKWOOD, JERRY RYAN, GEORGE DEIS
Old Forge, 1930, P061643

**THE FIRST CHRISTMAS TREE SET UP AT TIMES SQUARE IN
NEW YORK CITY, GIVEN BY THE ADIRONDACK LEAGUE CLUB**
Little Moose Lake, ca 1910, P000821

LOG HOUSE AT THE HEAD OF THIRD LAKE
Third Lake, ca 1875, P028631

ON BOARD A STEAMBOAT ON FOURTH LAKE
Eagle Bay, 1898, P061580

GIRLS AT THE MOSS LAKE CAMP
Moss Lake, ca 1935, P043155

MOSS LAKE CAMP LEAN-TO GATHERING
Moss Lake, ca 1935, P044180

HIGBY CAMP DINING ROOM
Big Moose, ca 1920, Frederick A. Hodges, P031633

BURDICK'S SUMMER HOUSE
Big Moose, ca 1910,
Henry M. Beach, P002809

**RAYMOND PARSON AND AMY ELIZABETH SISSON HONEYMOON
AT SEVENTH LAKE AFTER THEIR AUGUST 11, 1920, MARRIAGE**
Inlet, 1920, P061584

PORTRAIT OF WILLIAM WEST DURANT
ca 1884, Record & Epler, P018602

ECHO CAMP, BUILT IN 1883 FOR GOVERNOR LOUNSBURY OF CONNECTICUT
Raquette Lake, ca 1885, Alonzo L. Mix, P000079

RAILROAD MAGNATE AND DEVELOPER THOMAS DURANT
STANDING ON THE CORNER OF THE PORCH AT CAMP PINE KNOT
Raquette Lake, ca 1885, P020129

A HUDSON AUTOMOBILE CROSSING RAQUETTE LAKE ON A FERRY
Raquette Lake, 1915, P010889

OPEN AIR DINING ROOM AT CAMP PINE KNOT
Raquette Lake, ca 1880, Seneca Ray Stoddard, P001602

GUIDE CHAUNCEY HATHORN
RAN A TOURIST CAMP
ON GOLDEN BEACH
Raquette Lake, ca 1870, P007165

DR. SWEET, THE BONESETTER, AT INMAN CAMP
Raquette Lake, ca 1890, P008083

ALFRED VANDERBILT AND GUESTS ON TOBOGGANS AT SAGAMORE LODGE
Raquette Lake, ca 1910, P030741

COLLIER PRIVATE CLUB HOUSE
Raquette Lake, ca 1910, Alfred Santway, P017444

SAGAMORE LODGE DINING ROOM
Raquette Lake, 1949, P006892

MR. & MRS. LAURENCE LURNURE JR. HAVING TEA
Raquette Lake, 1893, Alonzo L. Mix, P011559

NORTHERN
REGION

AT NEWTON FALLS ABOVE THE DAM
Newton Falls, ca 1910, Henry M. Beach, P002469

IMMENCE PILE OF PULPWOOD — NEWTON FALLS, N.Y.

PULPWOOD AT NEWTON FALLS PAPER COMPANY
Newton Falls, ca 1910, Henry M. Beach, P002465

LOCOMOTIVE PUSHING ORE CARTS TO THE CRUSHER
Star Lake, ca 1910, Henry M. Beach, P002682

NILLS COTTAGE AND BOATHOUSE
Star Lake, ca 1910, Henry M. Beach, P002260

WHERE THE ORE IS CRUSHED, LARGEST ROLLER IN THE WORLD
BENSON MINES, N.Y.

BENSON IRON ORE MINES
Star Lake, ca 1910, Henry M. Beach, P002821

TRAIN AT WANEKENA STATION
Wanekena, ca 1905, P014917

**THE *WANAKENA*, OWNED BY THE RICH LUMBER COMPANY,
LETS OFF PASSENGERS AT NUNN'S INN DOCK**
Cranberry Lake, ca 1900, P011598

LAYING THE RAILS FOR THE GRASSE RIVER RAILROAD
Cranberry Lake, ca 1910, Henry M. Beach, P030757

ST. PAUL ROMAN CATHOLIC CHURCH
Piercefield, ca 1910, Henry M. Beach, P002954

BELL TELEPHONE COMPANY LINE ON TOP OF MT. ARAB
Piercefield, 1912, P061406

LABOR DAY PARADE
Piercefield, ca 1905, Frank J. McCormick, P038350

THE INTERNATIONAL HOTEL AND MAIN STREET FROM THE EAST
Piercefield, ca 1920, P009252

GEORGE MCCAULEY, DRIVER; EDWARD STAFFORD;
TOM BESAW, STANDING BY HORSES; DICK LEARY ON LOGS
Piercefield, 1899, McCormick Studios, P011357

HOTEL ALTAMONT, C.E. PIERSON PROPRIETOR
Tupper Lake, ca 1910, P038369

LINEMEN HANGING ON A TELEPHONE POLE, WITH MAID'S PHARMACY AT LEFT AND LEONARD AND LAROCQUE DRY GOODS AND SHOES AT RIGHT
Tupper Lake, ca 1915,
Henry M. Beach, P002924

E.B. GOUSLING ENJOYING HIMSELF AT KILDARE CAMP
Tupper Lake, 1912, P042705

ALTAMONT HOTEL BARBER SHOP, SILAS IVES, BARBER
Tupper Lake, 1900, P012891

GUIDE AT REST, A.A. LOW ESTATE
Tupper Lake, ca 1930, P020854

MEGGS LUMBER CO. ESTATE, FOLLENSBY POND
Tupper Lake, 1906, P012886

TUPPER LAKE HOUSE
Tupper Lake, 1890, Seneca Ray Stoddard, P027918

LINN TRACTOR, OVAL WOOD DISH CORPORATION
Tupper Lake, 1931, P047962

INTERIOR OF OVAL WOOD DISH MANUFACTURING CORPORATION
Tupper Lake, 1940, Frank McCormick, P062827

A PARADE THROUGH DOWNTOWN TUPPER LAKE
Tupper Lake, ca 1915, Frank J. McCormick, P038366

LAUNCHING AT THE OUTLET
Upper Saranac Lake, ca 1890, Seneca Ray Stoddard, P001320

VIEW OF ADOLPH LEWISOHN'S PROSPECT POINT CAMP FROM THE BOATHOUSE
Upper Saranac Lake, ca 1904, P038251

BOATHOUSE AT PROSPECT POINT CAMP
Upper Saranac Lake, ca 1904, P038250

GAME ROOM AT PROSPECT POINT CAMP
Upper Saranac Lake, ca 1904, P038249

WAWBEEK LODGE
Upper Saranac Lake, 1891, Seneca Ray Stoddard, P027952

CHILD ON A RAFT AT THE BIRCHES
Upper Saranac Lake, 1908, Frank Firth Hord, P022325

CHILDREN OF FRED WILLIAM RICE: (BACK ROW) FRED, JENNIE, ERNA, HATTIE, GEORGE; (FRONT ROW) LIZZIE, FANNIE, HERMAN, TILLIE, WILLIAM
Lower Saranac Lake, ca 1890, Fred William Rice, P038444

AMPERSAND HOTEL
Lower Saranac Lake, 1888, P027898

SERVICE STAFF
Lower Saranac Lake, ca 1900,
E.T. Start, P036464

**ALBERT EINSTEIN AND STATE SENATOR JOHN J. DUNNIGAN
AT THE SENATOR'S SUMMER HOME**
Lower Saranac Lake, 1936, P045078

COTTAGES AT THE TRUDEAU SANATORIUM
Saranac Lake, ca 1905, P022357

TRUDEAU SANATORIUM PATIENTS OUT SNOWSHOEING
Saranac Lake, 1890, Seneca Ray Stoddard, P037899

TUBERCULOSIS PATIENTS TAKING THE CURE AT THE TRUDEAU SANATORIUM
Saranac Lake, ca 1892, Seneca Ray Stoddard, P028028

FOX MOVIETONE NEWS TRUCK
Saranac Lake, 1929, William F. Kollecker, P059011

HUNTING AND FISHING WITH MISS PRATT AND M.E. CONKLIN
Saranac Lake, ca 1905, Raymond Blauvelt, P028906

WINTER CARNIVAL ICE PALACE
Saranac Lake, ca 1910, P021023

D.T. BUCKLEY MOVING PICTURE CAMP
Saranac Lake, ca 1913, P035584

NEW YORK CENTRAL DEPOT IN THE ADIRONDACKS
Saranac Lake, ca 1890, P006895

THE STATION AND SHELTER AT LAKE CLEAR JUNCTION,
MOHAWK & MALONE RAILROAD #10
Lake Clear Junction, ca 1900, P006745

LAKE CLEAR INN

Lake Clear, ca 1920, Eastern Illustrating Co., P012266

COZY COTTAGES AT LAKE CLEAR INN

Lake Clear, 1910, P002240

MARJORIE MERRIWEATHER POST'S CAMP TOPRIDGE
Upper St. Regis Lake, ca 1960, P068564

LIVING ROOM AT TOPRIDGE
Upper St. Regis Lake, 1959, P068589

BOATHOUSE ON BIRCH ISLAND LANDING, HOOKER CAMP
Upper St. Regis Lake, ca 1890, P020160

ELLA REID HARRISON'S SLEEPING TENT AT WILD AIR, A PRIVATE CAMP
Upper St. Regis Lake, 1882, P011423

VIEW FROM ST. REGIS MOUNTAIN OF OSGOOD POND, JONES POND, PAUL SMITH'S, UPPER ST. REGIS LAKE, SPECTACLE POND, SPITFIRE LAKE, AND LOWER ST. REGIS LAKE
Upper St. Regis, ca 1890, Seneca Ray Stoddard, P001360

GUIDE HOUSE AT PAUL SMITH'S HOTEL
Lower St. Regis Lake, ca 1880, Seneca Ray Stoddard, P024173

PORTRAIT OF PAUL SMITH,
EARLY ADIRONDACK
DEVELOPER
Lower St. Regis Lake, 1878,
Seneca Ray Stoddard, P015202

PRESIDENT CALVIN COOLIDGE WITH PAUL SMITH'S SON PHELPS SMITH
AT WHITE PINE CAMP, THE SUMMER WHITE HOUSE
Osgood Pond, 1926, P044982

MAIN STREET, IGA STORE
Onchiota, ca 1920, Eastern Illustrating Co., P012614

A FINE GROUP OF STUDENTS, ST. REGIS FALLS SCHOOL
St. Regis Falls, ca 1910, Henry M. Beach, P002211

THE CHATEAUGAY HOUSE, ALSO CALLED THE OWLYOUT HOTEL, FROM THE SOUTH
Chateaugay, ca 1895, Seneca Ray Stoddard, P028018

CHARCOAL KILNS, THE NARROWS
Chateaugay Lake, 1891, Seneca Ray Stoddard, P001729

**SIGNAL STATION NEAR
LYON MOUNTAIN**
*Lyon Mountain, 1883,
Verplanck Colvin, P007537*

Lake Champlain
Region

LAKE VIEW HOUSE
Ausable Chasm, ca 1880, P033010

RUNNING THE RAPIDS
Ausable Chasm, ca 1880, Seneca Ray Stoddard, P049254

CYCLISTS AT DEVIL'S OVEN
Ausable Chasm, ca 1888, George W. Baldwin, P006684

KEESEVILLE, AUSABLE CHASM & LAKE CHAMPLAIN RAILROAD
CROSSING THE TRESSLE AT AUSABLE CHASM
Ausable Chasm, 1890, P069443

DEER'S HEAD INN
Elizabethtown, ca 1935, P041480

WINDSOR HOUSE
Elizabethtown, ca 1889, Seneca Ray Stoddard, P026933

MANSION HOUSE
Elizabethtown, ca 1880, Seneca Ray Stoddard, P027665

JACK'S CAMP BENEATH THE PINES
Elizabethtown, ca 1930, Eastern Illustrating Co., P013532

LISLE COUNTIN BUILDING
Elizabethtown, ca 1935, Alfred Santway, P041476

IRON MINERS IN JOKER MINE
Mineville, ca 1907, P047737

LAKE CHAMPLAIN AND MOIRA RAILROAD
Port Henry, ca 1910, Henry M. Beach, P006242

FOOTE BLOCK
Port Henry, ca 1910, P023531

PORT HENRY BUSINESS DISTRICT
Port Henry, ca 1910, Henry M. Beach, P003719

PORT HENRY LANDING
Port Henry, ca 1910, Henry M. Beach, P003733

MINE SHAFT
Port Henry, ca 1900, S.A. Noves, P048171

BRIDGE ACROSS LAKE CHAMPLAIN
Crown Point, ca 1920, P013508

TICONDEROGA RAILROAD DOCK
Ticonderoga, 1881, Seneca Ray Stoddard, P027004

FORT TICONDEROGA RUINS, INTERIOR OFFICERS QUARTERS
Ticonderoga, 1871, Seneca Ray Stoddard, P032989

HIGH PEAKS REGION

TAKING PHOTOS FROM THE SUMMIT OF MT. MARCY
High Peaks, 1908, Norman Stewart Foote, P023340

"When signs fail," Bob Marshall in the High Peaks
High Peaks, 1925, George Marshall, P049032

Dix Mountain and Hunter's Pass from Noonmark Mountain
High Peaks, 1925, Francis L. Bayle, P015757

**INDIAN HEAD, LOWER AUSABLE
LAKE (C.O. BEEDE GUIDEBOAT)**
*High Peaks, 1889, Seneca Ray Stoddard,
P026705*

**HIKERS FROM PUTNAM CAMP SPELL OUT "MARCY" ON
THE SUMMIT OF NEW YORK'S HIGHEST PEAK**
High Peaks, 1902, H.P. Bowditch, P049740

**JOHNS BROOK ON THE WAY
TOWARD MOUNT MARCY**
High Peaks, 1927, P059409

GATEWAY TO THE ADIRONDACK MOUNTAIN RESERVE, SAINT HUBERT'S INN
Keene Valley, 1891, Seneca Ray Stoddard, P015184

**THE AUSABLE LAKE STAGE LINE IN FRONT OF THE
MAIN ENTRANCE TO THE ADIRONDACK HOUSE**
Keene Valley, 1889, Seneca Ray Stoddard, P027931

WILMINGTON NOTCH, AUSABLE RIVER
Keene, ca 1935, G.T. Rabineau, P041544

ARTISTS ON THE AUSABLE RIVER
INCLUDING ROSWELL M.
SHURTLEFF (FRONT CENTER),
WINSLOW HOMER (WITH PIPE
IN SECOND ROW), CALVIN RAE
SMITH, AND KRUSEMAN
VANELTEN
Keene, 1874, J.F. Murphy, P047500

OLD MOUNTAIN PHELPS, PIONEER GUIDE
Keene, ca 1890, F.J. Franklyn, P068128

OLYMPIC ARENA, WILLIAM DISTIN, ARCHITECT
Lake Placid, 1932, P038234

GRECIAN BALLET IN MID-SUMMER FIGURE SKATING OPERETTA, OLYMPIC ARENA
Lake Placid, ca 1935, Pierson Studio, P041514

US Olympic Team, 1932 Olympic Winter Games Opening Ceremony
Lake Placid, 1932, P042058

Winter fun at Mirror Lake
Lake Placid, ca 1925, P035557

GRAND VIEW HOUSE
Lake Placid, 1893, Seneca Ray Stoddard, P015327

THE OFFICE OF GRAND VIEW HOTEL, FORMERLY GRAND VIEW HOUSE
Lake Placid, ca 1910, Henry M. Beach, P003138

THE *DORIS* LEAVING THE GEORGE & BLISS DOCK
Lake Placid, ca 1935, Alfred Santway, P041503

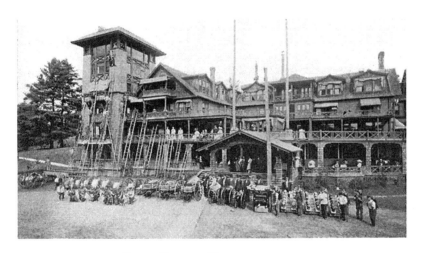

LAKE PLACID CLUB FIRE DRILL
Lake Placid, 1914, Adirondack Museum Library

WHITEFACE INN
Lake Placid, ca 1935, Alfred Santway, P041534

SUMMER VIEW OF NORTH ELBA
Lake Placid, ca 1890, Seneca Ray Stoddard, P007919

WHITEFACE MOUNTAIN
Lake Placid, ca 1935, P041553

COL. CHARLES LINDBERGH AT LAKE PLACID, SATURDAY, AUGUST 13, 1939
Lake Placid, 1939, William F. Kollecker, P058902

CENTRAL

REGION

NEWCOMB VILLAGE
Newcomb, 1912, P015716

LAKE HARRIS HOUSE
Newcomb, 1908, Norman Stewart Foote, P023236

SPAIN'S STORE, POST OFFICE, AND RESIDENCE
Newcomb, Eastern Illustrating Co., ca 1910, P042000

**NOAH LaCASSE, TAHAWUS CLUB GUIDE
AND THEODORE ROOSEVELT'S GUIDE**
Newcomb, ca 1910, P014847

BLAST FURNACE, MacINTYRE MINES, TAHAWUS
Newcomb, ca 1875, Seneca Ray Stoddard, P048468

LONG LAKE VILLAGE
Long Lake, ca 1920, Eastern Illustrating Co., P012397

MITCHELL SABATTIS,
ADIRONDACK GUIDE
Long Lake, ca 1860, D.S. Brush, P009318

**ADIRONDACK HERMIT
NOAH JOHN RONDEAU,
COLD RIVER CITY**
Long Lake, ca 1950, P029059

LONG LAKE HOTEL
Long Lake, ca 1890, P022798

ARTHUR FITZWILLIAM TAIT'S HOUSEBOAT,
USED TO PAINT, FISH, HUNT, AND SLEEP FROM 1872 TO 1882
Long Lake, ca 1882, P023780

BUTTERMILK (PHANTOM) FALLS
Long Lake, 1898, P023417

LONG VIEW LODGE BOAT LAUNCH
Long Lake, ca 1910, Henry M. Beach, P002153

NE-HA-SA-NE LODGE
Lake Lila, 1902, T.E. Marr, P023728

NE-HA-SA-NE LODGE AND BOATHOUSE
Lake Lila, ca 1900, P045683

INTERIOR OF CAMP GOOD ENOUGH
Brandreth Park, ca 1890, P000844

TROPHY LODGE
Brandreth Park, ca 1910,
Henry M. Beach,
P002024

THE CHAMPION LOAD OF LOGS
Brandreth Park, ca 1910, Henry M. Beach, P019513

**OUTING AT BRANDRETH PARK, GUIDE REUBEN CARY (LEFT)
AND INEZ CARY (WITH FISHING POLE AND CREEL)**
Brandreth Park, ca 1885, P042763

CAMP CEDARS
Forked Lake, ca 1880, Seneca Ray Stoddard, P019075

INTERIOR OF CAMP CEDARS
Forked Lake, ca 1890, F. Clark Durant Jr., P019984

HOLLAND'S BLUE MOUNTAIN HOUSE
Blue Mountain Lake, ca 1890, Edward Bierstadt, P001549

PROSPECT HOUSE
Blue Mountain Lake, ca 1885 P066409

INTERIOR OF PROSPECT HOUSE
Blue Mountain Lake, ca 1890, Edward Bierstadt, P001027

BOATS *TOWAHLOONDAH* AND *IROCOSIA* AT THE MARION RIVER CARRY
Blue Mountain Lake, ca 1880, P006965

PRIVATE COTTAGES NEAR BLUE MOUNTAIN HOUSE, INCLUDING
BULL COTTAGE, HAVEN CAMP, INGERSOLL CAMP, WILLIAMS-WERNER CAMP,
WERNER CAMP, LOVE CAMP, AND CAMP KILCORAWAH
Blue Mountain Lake, ca 1915, Elmer E. Kellogg, P015421

RAILROAD AT MARION RIVER CARRY
Blue Mountain Lake, ca 1900, P060935

BLUE MOUNTAIN LAKE SCHOOL WITH TEACHER LILIAS CROSS AND STUDENTS
Blue Mountain Lake, ca 1939, P059224

CURRY'S RESTAURANT
Blue Mountain Lake, ca 1910, Eastern Illustrating Co., P011894

A COZY NOOK IN WEST BAY
Blue Mountain Lake, ca 1900, Edward Bierstadt, P006777

BLUE MOUNTAIN HOUSE, PRESENT-DAY SITE OF THE ADIRONDACK MUSEUM
Blue Mountain Lake, P066403